The Power of
a Single Thought

The Power of
a Single Thought

How to Initiate Major Life Changes
from the Quiet of Your Mind

A New Interpretation of James Allen's
Transformational Classic
As a Man Thinketh

REVISED AND EDITED BY GAY HENDRICKS
AND DEBBIE DEVOE

HAY HOUSE, INC.
Carlsbad, California • New York City
London • Sydney • New Delhi

Published in the United States by: Hay House, Inc.: www.hayhouse.com
Published in Australia by: Hay House Australia Pty. Ltd.: www.hayhouse.com.au
Published in the United Kingdom by: Hay House UK, Ltd.: www.hayhouse.co.uk
Published in India by: Hay House Publishers India: www.hayhouse.co.in

Editorial supervision: Jill Kramer • *Design:* Tricia Breidenthal

Library of Congress Control No.: 2005921157

ISBN: 978-1-4019-6833-5

1st printing, February 2006
3rd printing, January 2008

Printed in the United States of America

*We dedicate this work to the
memory of James Allen,
in gratitude for the millions of lives
his loving words have touched.*

CONTENTS

PART III: THE ORIGINAL VERSION OF *AS A MAN THINKETH*

INTRODUCTION

CHANGE ONE THOUGHT AND YOU CHANGE YOUR LIFE

As you think, so you are. This aphorism sums up one of the most significant principles in psychological and spiritual growth. William James, the founder of American psychology, said that the most important discovery of his time is that you can improve your life simply by changing the quality of your thoughts. He lived in the great 19th century, when telephones, steam engines, and other remarkable machines were invented, so he was paying a high compliment to this concept.

Thousands of years ago the Buddha said it this way: Everything we are arises with our thoughts. This concept is found in the Bible, in the Hindu sacred literature, and in the basic tenets of most of the world's religions. And one major practical reason for the universality of this concept is that you don't need any outside help to change your thoughts; you can do it instantly, and you can do it anytime you want. Knowing these simple truths gives you a tremendous power that comes completely from within.

Many notions come into your mind completely unbidden. That's one way your mind works; it just pumps out thought after thought without your doing anything at all—much as your heart beats without your having to remind it to do so every second. You don't always have direct control over what pops into your mind, but you *do* have complete control over what you consciously insert into your thought stream. That's why the principle "As you think, so you are" has such extraordinary power.

For example, you might find yourself spontaneously entertaining a thought that you don't want to affirm anymore. As soon as that happens, you can decide to change the direction of that thought stream by consciously inserting a new idea. The old, negative notion might continue to show up from time to time, but now you've made a fundamental alteration in the program that's been running your mind. Thus, your conscious effort to think positively has effected change within you.

That's why every one of the spiritual teachers, motivational speakers, and inspirational authors we've interviewed over the years has recommended one or more books on the subject of changing your thoughts. The most frequently mentioned of all is the classic *As a Man Thinketh* by James Allen, first written 100 years ago, which we've edited and interpreted anew for modern seekers.

The book you're holding has changed the lives of thousands—perhaps millions—of people, since its publication in the Victorian era. Unfortunately, many readers in modern times have not been able to access the book's remarkable power because of the stilted language in which it was originally written. Since this book is so crucial to understanding the true makeup of the human mind, we've attempted to express its timeless principles in modern language so that everyone can benefit from the concepts within it.

Our intention with this new version is to bring this remarkable book to readers of a new millennium, free of the sometimes stiff, sexist diction of Allen's time. Our hope is that our efforts to modernize the book will preserve and even enhance its power so that today's seeker will be able to harvest the rich benefits of this classic work without being hindered by the limitations of outdated language. Readers who wish to compare our efforts with Allen's original version will find it in Part III of this work.

May this transformational jewel mean as much to you as it has to us, Neale Donald Walsch, and the countless others who have savored its central idea and used it to change their lives.

— **Gay Hendricks, Ph.D.**, and **Debbie DeVoe**

PART I

A New Interpretation of *As a Man Thinketh*

Chapter One

How You Think
Is Who You Are

The saying "As you think, so you are" holds true for every part of your being and every aspect of your life. You are what you think, with your character being the complete and direct result of your beliefs. Just as a plant springs from the same seed that it requires to exist, your actions also grow from the hidden seeds of your thoughts and couldn't occur without them. Action is the blossom of those thoughts, and joy and suffering are its fruits.

What you *think* makes you who you *are*. So if your thoughts are negative, then you'll experience pain; if positive, you'll experience joy. In other words, based on the quality of the thoughts you entertain—both spontaneous and deliberate—you'll harvest sweet or bitter fruits.

Your character is governed by natural laws, including the law of cause and effect, which is just as applicable and inescapable when it comes to the intangible workings of your mind as it is for the visible, physical world around you. Your character isn't virtuous and magnificent because of special favor or chance—no, these character traits are the direct result of consciously choosing to be positive. By the same token, if you continually dwell on the negative, your character will be inferior and degraded.

You create who you are, and you can change who you are with a single thought. You can turn your thoughts into weapons that you use to destroy yourself, or you can turn them into tools you use to build joy, strength, and peace. By consciously choosing to think positively, you live divinely. By engaging in negative thinking, you live wretchedly. All grades of character exist between these two extremes. It's up to you to choose the quality of your convictions, and thereby create the character you desire.

Of all the incredible truths we've learned about the soul, none is more empowering than this: *You* are the master of your thoughts and the creator of your character. You make and shape who you are, the world you live in, and your destiny. You're always in control—even if you make poor choices. And as a powerful, intelligent, and loving person who is the master of your own thinking, you hold the key to transforming every situation. At any given moment, you can turn yourself into whomever you want to be.

Unconscious thoughts will occur naturally, but it's up to you to monitor the quality of your thinking when you become aware of it. When you actually notice a specific negative notion, you can consciously insert a positive new belief into your thought stream. For example, you might see a man or woman you'd like to meet and automatically think, *I can't go up and talk to that person. I never have anything interesting to say.* But since you're in control of your own mind, you can replace that idea with a powerful, positive affirmation that will likely lead to a more fruitful action, such as, *I'm going to introduce myself. I bet we have a lot in common.*

It's your choice to be a wise or foolish master of your mind. If you want to be wise, then you must use your thoughts to intelligently direct your actions and energies. With some practice you'll be able to watch, control, and modify your pattern of thinking in order to mold your life to your liking. You'll also be able to track the effect of your beliefs on yourself, on others, and on your life and circumstances, proving that you're truly the maker of your character and the creator of your destiny.

As you patiently investigate the cause and effect of your thoughts in every situation—even in the most trivial, everyday occurrence—you'll gain self-knowledge, wisdom, and power. Through continued self-analysis, experience, and awareness, you'll become a conscious master who learns every truth within you. With some practice and dedication, you'll discover the absolute law that those who seek . . . find doors open to those who knock.

Chapter Two

How Your Thoughts Shape Your Life

Your mind is like a garden that you can cultivate intelligently or allow to run wild. Whether cared for or neglected, the garden will grow. But if no useful seeds are planted, many undesirable ones will fall into the fertile ground, and weeds will take root.

Just as gardeners cultivate their plots, keeping them free of nettles and thorns and growing the flowers and fruits they desire, you can tend to the garden of your mind. You can uproot all your negative, useless beliefs and consciously nurture powerful, positive thoughts instead. By doing so, you'll eventually discover that you're the master gardener of your soul and the director of your life. You'll also come to comprehend the laws of thought, and with ever-increasing accuracy, understand how the workings of your mind shape your character, life circumstances, and destiny.

Thought and character are one. Because your character can only manifest itself outwardly, the outer conditions of your life will always mirror your inner state. This doesn't mean that the circumstances of your life at any given time are a reflection of your entire character; it means that whatever you're going through is intimately connected with some vital thought element within you, which is, at least for the time being, indispensable to your development.

You are where you are by the law of your being, and the thoughts that have built your character have brought you to this point. Chance plays no role whatsoever in the circumstances of your existence—it's all the result of an unerring law. This is just as true for people who feel a sense of alienation with their surroundings as it is for those who are in harmonious balance.

Your life's circumstances are what they are so that you can grow, allowing you to forever evolve and progress as a person. As you learn the spiritual lesson contained for you in each chapter, that phase passes away and makes room for a new set of conditions.

Circumstance will knock you around as long as you believe that you're a slave to outside forces. When you realize that you're a creative power in your own right and that you have control over the hidden thoughts out of which the conditions of your life arise, then you'll become the rightful master of yourself.

Anyone who's practiced self-control and positive thinking for any length of time knows that "destiny" grows out of thought. Improvements in your situation occur in exact proportion to the transformation of the quality of your state of mind. You'll find that when you earnestly apply yourself to bettering your character and replacing negative thoughts with positive ones, you'll quickly see improvements in your relationships, work, health, and overall demeanor.

The Law of Attraction

You attract whatever you spend time pondering, including whatever you love and whatever you fear. Your soul will rise to achieve your highest hope and will also fall to the depths of your basest appetite—and your life will be a direct reflection of all your desires. This holds true for both your conscious and unconscious thoughts, which may seem a bit confusing at first. For example, you may want prosperity and believe that you're working toward bringing more of it into your life. Your savings account, however, remains empty. This is because unconsciously you're thinking, *I'm afraid of poverty, and I don't think I'll ever be rich.* Even though you've made an effort to increase your wealth, your pessimistic thinking with respect to money is so ingrained that it actually cancels out your positive steps. Yet with continued effort and vigilance against negative self-talk, you can turn around and create a prosperous life.

The outer world of your circumstances is shaped by the inner world of your thoughts. Every seed of thought that you sow or allow to fall into your mind and take root eventually blossoms into action. And once again, good thoughts bear sweet fruit, while bad ones bear rotten fruit. A person doesn't end up homeless or in jail by the tyranny of fate or by chance, but as the direct result of cynical thinking and corrupt desires. Similarly, a model citizen doesn't suddenly commit a crime due to a chance occurrence, but because he or she secretly fostered the criminal thought for a long time.

Again, circumstance doesn't create who you are. Instead, it reveals you to yourself. If your life isn't what you want it to be or is filled with suffering, it's because of your antagonistic thinking. If your life is exactly what you want and is filled with joy, it's because you're continually cultivating a hopeful mind-set. As the master of your self, you're responsible for shaping and creating your life. From birth forward, you learn through both suffering and joy, and the purity or impurity of your thoughts determine the condition of your life, reflecting the strength or weakness of your soul.

You don't attract what you *want,* but what you actually *are.* At any moment, your thoughts can thwart your whims, desires, and ambitions—leaving your savings account empty even though you want to be rich, or leaving you single even though you dream of a loving marriage. The concept of a divinity that shapes your life is within you; in fact, that divinity is your very self. You are the only one who can hold you back. Your thoughts and actions can be the jailers of your fate, imprisoning you with shame. On the other hand, your thoughts and actions can be your angels, freeing you to create whatever you want through their goodness. You see, you don't receive what you wish and pray for, but what you justly *earn.* Your wishes and prayers are only answered when they harmonize with positive thoughts and actions.

In light of this truth, you may ask what it means when people are said to be "fighting against fate." This simply refers to those who continually struggle with an outer effect while inwardly nourishing and preserving a negative cause in their hearts, whether it be a conscious vice or an unconscious weakness. Whatever it is, the root of the problem stubbornly prevents these people from attaining what they really want, and leaves them fighting against the circumstances they've created.

People are usually anxious to improve their lot in life, but are much less willing to improve themselves. As a result, they're often unfulfilled. If you rise to the task of continually banishing negative thinking, you'll achieve whatever your heart and mind desire. This is true for both physical and spiritual things.

Imagine a poor man who desperately wants to improve his physical circumstances. The problem is that he doesn't show up for work, justifying his laziness by saying that he isn't getting paid enough to make an effort. This sort of person doesn't understand anything about the basic principles of prosperity. Not only is he totally incapable of rising out of his wretchedness, but he also digs himself into a deeper hole by constantly complaining and passively waiting for someone else to do the work for him.

And what about the rich woman who suffers from a painful, chronic disease caused by her excess weight?

She's willing to pay lavishly to treat the disease, but isn't willing to refrain from overeating. She wants to gorge herself on any food she desires and still feel vibrant. Such a person is totally unfit for wellness because she hasn't learned the first principles of a healthy lifestyle.

Finally, there's the business owner who cheats her employees out of a fair wage in order to make a larger profit. When she finds herself bankrupt—both in terms of reputation and riches—she blames circumstances, not understanding that she's the sole creator of her condition.

I've introduced these examples to illustrate the truth that *you* are the creator of *your* existence, although your circumstances are nearly always formed unconsciously. Even if you have a positive goal in mind, you'll continually fail to achieve it if you foster thoughts and desires that conflict with your intended end result. I could present an infinite number of examples, but this isn't necessary. If you're willing, you can trace the cause and effect of your beliefs on your own experiences. Once you've done so, you can really begin to evaluate your own life.

(However, because circumstances are so complicated, your thoughts are so deeply rooted, and the foundation of happiness varies so greatly for different people, the condition of your entire soul—although it may be known to you—can't be judged by someone else solely on the basis of the external aspects of your life.)

Positive Thoughts Always Equal Positive Results

Some people will argue that we're all at the mercy of chance, because there are honest folks out there who still lack basic necessities and comforts, while the dishonest acquire wealth. This is really a misperception based on a superficial judgment that assumes that those who are dishonest are usually totally corrupt, and that honest people are wholly virtuous. In the light of deeper knowledge and wider experience, it's now known that this assumption is incorrect. A dishonest person may have some admirable qualities that an honest person doesn't possess, and an honest person may have some obnoxious vices that are absent in a dishonest person. Just people reap the good results of their honorable thoughts and acts, and they also bring upon themselves the sufferings that result from their vices. Likewise, shady characters merit their own joy and pain.

Because of our vanity, we like to believe that we suffer because of our virtues. However, until you purge every sick, bitter, and negative thought from your mind and wash every stain from your soul, you can't be in a position to know and declare that your sufferings are the result of your good—and not your bad—qualities. On your way to supreme perfection (but long before you attain it), you'll discover that the law of thought is absolutely just by seeing firsthand how the quality of your thoughts impact your life. This law simply doesn't allow good to result from evil and evil to result from good. Once you possess this knowledge, you can look back on your past ignorance and blindness and see that your life is and always has been perfectly ordered: All of your past experiences, pleasing or painful, were the direct result of your evolving self.

Positive thoughts and actions can never generate negative results, just as negative thoughts and actions can never bring forth positive results. In the same way, a flower can't beget anything but more flowers, and a weed can't produce anything but more weeds. We all understand this law in the natural world, but few of us understand this law in the realm of the mind and morals—even though its operation is just as simple and undeviating.

Suffering is always the effect of some sort of counter-productive thinking. It's a sign that you're out of harmony with yourself and with the law of your existence. The sole and supreme use of suffering is to purify, burning out all that is useless and negative. But suffering ceases once you become pure. Just as there's no reason to keep scalding a tomato once you've removed the skin, a perfectly pure and enlightened person can't suffer.

You can choose to approach your circumstances from a positive or negative perspective. Happiness, not material possession, is the measure of an optimistic mind-set; a sorrowful existence, not lack of material possession, is the measure of pessimism. You may be depressed and rich, or you may be cheerful and poor, since joy and wealth only come together when people use their riches rightly and wisely. Wretchedness and poverty go hand in hand when people regard their lot in life as an unjustly imposed burden. People don't achieve their full magnificence until they're happy, healthy, and prosperous—with their happiness, health, and prosperity resulting from a harmonious balance between their inner life and their outer surroundings.

You only truly fulfill your potential when you stop complaining about your circumstances and search for the hidden logic that regulates your existence. Once you understand this, you stop blaming others for whatever has gone wrong in your life, and you improve your character by cultivating positive thoughts. You also stop fighting your outward conditions and progress more rapidly by discovering the hidden powers and possibilities within yourself.

Law, not confusion, is the dominating principle in the universe. Justice, not inequity, is the soul and substance of life. Righteousness, not corruption, is the force that molds the spiritual government of the world. This being so, you'll find that all is right in the universe if you right yourself. During this process of improving yourself, you'll also find that as you transform your thoughts toward things and other people, your relationships with things and other people will evolve. The proof of this truth is in every person; you can easily test it through systematic introspection and self-analysis. If you radically alter your thoughts, you'll be astonished at the rapid transformation that will occur in the material conditions of your life.

People think they can hide their thoughts, but they can't. Thoughts rapidly become habits, and habits create your life's conditions. Negative thoughts of every kind—including fear, doubt, indecision, laziness, meanness, blame, and hate—turn into energy-sapping, debilitating vices. These vices in turn create adverse circumstances, including failure, destitution, slavish dependence, violence, addiction, and disease. Conversely, positive thoughts of all kinds—including courage, kindness, decisiveness, temperance, forgiveness, and love—crystallize into energetic, empowering virtues. These virtues in turn create favorable circumstances, including success, plentitude, ease, peace, health, and freedom.

Persistent positive or negative thinking about a given issue will certainly impact your character and your life. You can't directly choose your circumstances, but you can choose your thoughts. By doing so, you can indirectly, yet surely, shape your experience. The universe will bring opportunities your way based on the quality of your thinking, and if you stop dwelling in negativity, the entire world will be ready to help you, and opportunities will abound to support your positive resolve.

You can be whatever you want. Your spirit is free. You are the master of time and space, and fate and chance hold no power over you. By directing the power of your will, you can achieve any goal you want, even in the face of enormous obstacles. Don't lose your resolve if change doesn't happen immediately. Be patient, knowing that you're the master of yourself and your life. When you direct your power in positive ways, the world will shift to support you!

Chapter Three

How Your Thoughts
Impact Your Health

Your body is your mind's servant, and it obeys the workings of your mind—including your conscious thoughts, hidden desires, and automatic reflexes. If you dwell in negativity, you'll quickly sink into disease and decay. If you focus on upbeat, positive thoughts, you'll become youthful and beautiful.

Your body is a delicate, elastic instrument that readily responds to the thoughts impressed on it, whether good or bad. Ill thoughts express themselves through physical illness. In fact, fear has been known to kill a man as fast as a bullet—and it continually kills thousands of people just as surely, if less rapidly. If you live in fear of disease, you'll contract diseases, because anxiety quickly weakens your entire body, inviting illnesses in. Base thoughts, even if not acted upon, will soon destroy your nervous system. In contrast, strong, pure, and optimistic thoughts build vigorous, graceful bodies.

Your health will deteriorate as long as you foster negative thoughts. If you have a serene mind, you'll have a wholesome life and body—pessimism will ensure a miserable existence and physical ailments. Your thoughts are a fountain of actions, energy, and manifestation—take care of this fountain and all will be well. (You understand by now that simply eating a nutritious diet won't make you healthy if you don't change your thoughts. Besides, when you clean up your thoughts, you won't crave junk food.)

Optimistic thinking fosters beneficial habits. If you've strengthened and purified your thoughts, you've taken an important step in protecting yourself from disease. If you want to rejuvenate your body, then beautify your mind. Thoughts of malice, envy, disappointment, and dejection are what rob vitality and grace from your body.

A dour expression doesn't appear by chance; it's the result of unpleasant thoughts. Wrinkles that line your face are drawn by negative thought patterns. I know a

96-year-old woman who has the bright, innocent countenance of a young girl. I also know a man well under
middle age whose face is harsh and shriveled. One appear-
ance is the result of a kind and sunny disposition, while
the other is caused by meanness and dissatisfaction. Just
as you can't have an inviting, comfortable home unless
you let fresh air and sunshine into your rooms, a strong
body and a bright, happy, and peaceful countenance can
only result from the nurturing of joyful, positive, serene
thoughts.

Faces can be wrinkled by distress, brightened by pos-
itiveness, or carved by rage. Who can't tell the difference? For people who have focused on living joyously,
to grow old is to calmly, peacefully, and softly mellow
like the setting sun. I recently saw a philosopher on his
deathbed. He wasn't old except in years, and he died as
sweetly and peacefully as he'd lived.

There's no prescription like cheerful thought to cure
your body's illnesses, and there's no greater comfort than
benevolence to ease grief and sorrow. If you continually
live with thoughts of ill will, cynicism, suspicion, and

envy, you'll confine yourself to a self-made prison cell. But if each day you think well of all—being cheerful with everyone and patiently learning to find the good in every person and in every moment—you'll experience an abundance of peace.

Chapter Four

THE POWER OF PURPOSEFUL THOUGHT

Unless you link your thoughts with a clear purpose, you won't accomplish anything. You'll either allow your life to be the haphazard result of your undirected thought patterns, or you'll fail to follow through on achieving your goals.

Most people let the majority of their thoughts drift aimlessly, leading to catastrophe, destruction, or simple discontent. People who have no central purpose in their life are prone to petty worries, fears, dramas, and self-pity, which are all indications of weakness that lead to failure, unhappiness, and loss, just as surely as deliberate acts of wrongdoing.

You should define a clear purpose in your heart and then set out to accomplish your goal by making it the focal point of your thoughts. Your purpose may take the form of a spiritual ideal or a material object, but whatever it is, you should steadily focus on the objective you've set before you, making it your top priority. You should devote yourself to achieving it, not allowing your thoughts to wander away into wishful thinking and daydreaming.

This steady focus on a clear purpose is the ultimate path to self-control and true concentration. Even if you fail over and over to attain your goal (as will be the case until you overcome any weaknesses within you), the strength of character that you gain will be the measure of your genuine success, and this will form a new starting point for attaining future power and achievement.

If you feel overwhelmed by the idea of having such a singular purpose, you should focus your thoughts on doing the best you can in your daily activities, no matter how insignificant a given task may seem. In this way, over time you'll be able to hone in on what's important to you. By successfully completing everyday tasks, you'll learn how to concentrate your energies, and trust your ability to accomplish anything you put your mind to.

If an extremely weak person embraces the truth that strength can only be developed through dedication and practice and begins to make such an effort, this person's soul will grow and develop with each exertion until it becomes incredibly powerful. Just as physically weak people can make themselves strong through careful and patient training, so can people with weak wills make themselves steadfast by the practice of inserting positive affirmations into their thought stream.

When you turn away from aimlessness and weakness and begin to think with purpose, you enter the ranks of powerful people who understand that failure is one of the roads to success. These people think positively, using existing conditions to their benefit. They act without fear and masterfully accomplish whatever they desire.

Once you've identified your purpose, envision a straight path to its achievement, and follow this path without looking to the right or left. Vigilantly guard against thoughts of doubt and fear, as they'll distract you from your goal. Doubt and fear have never accomplished anything, and they never will—they always lead to failure. When doubt and fear creep into your mind, your positive thinking stops and your determination, energy, and power to achieve what you desire evaporates. This is why it's so important to link your thoughts to a purpose.

Take, for instance, your hypothetical desire to quit smoking. If one day you simply think to yourself, *I plan to quit smoking,* you're unlikely to succeed in your quest. Because you haven't tied a clear purpose to your thoughts and desires, you'll likely light up again the next time you're tempted by the sight of someone else enjoying a cigarette. But you know that if you decide to quit and you imbue this thought with purpose, you're much more likely to succeed. So you make a list of all the reasons why you're kicking the habit, and you commit to reviewing this list anytime you're tempted to smoke in the future. This sense of purpose and commitment helps you overcome temptation and push aside doubts and fears about succeeding. By planting seeds of purpose into your thought stream, you make it possible to harvest the ripe fruit of your desires instead of having them fall to the ground prematurely.

The will to succeed springs from the knowledge that you *can* succeed. Doubt and fear are the great enemies of self-knowledge. If you allow them to enter your thought stream and fail to guard against them, they'll trip you up at every step. If you conquer them, you conquer failure. Your every thought is infused with power, enabling you to overcome all obstacles with courage and wisdom.

Thought imbued with purpose becomes a creative force. When you truly understand this, you're ready to become something much more powerful than a useless bundle of wavering thoughts and fluctuating feelings. When you tie your intentions to a clear purpose, you gain the ability to wield your mental powers with intelligence and direction.

Chapter Five

HOW YOUR THOUGHTS
IMPACT YOUR SUCCESS

Everything you achieve and everything you fail to achieve is the direct result of your own thinking. You're completely responsible for your life. Your strengths and weaknesses are your own—created by your own hand and no one else's. You're also the only person who can change your character. Your suffering and happiness are created within you. How you think is who you are, and however you continue to think is who you'll continue to be.

Strong people can't help the weak unless they're willing to be helped. Even then, the weaker ones must lift themselves up by their own effort, eventually developing the strength they admire in others. Each of us is the only one who can change our character and life.

For centuries, people have said and believed the following: "Many people are slaves because one person oppresses them, so let's hate the oppressor." These days there's an increasing tendency to reverse this judgment and say that one person is an oppressor because many people are willing to be slaves, so the slaves are the ones to blame. The truth is that the oppressor and the slave *both* live in ignorance. While each seems to make the other suffer, in reality, they're creating their own anguish. A person who understands the law of thought sees how the oppressed create their own weakness and how oppressors misapply their power. A person capable of unconditional love sees the misery of both and condemns neither. A truly compassionate person embraces both the oppressor and the oppressed.

When you conquer your weaknesses and banish all negative thoughts, you're neither a tyrant nor a slave. You're free. You can rise, conquer, and achieve only by lifting up your thoughts. You remain weak, abject, and miserable only by refusing to elevate these thoughts.

Before you can achieve anything—even material things—you must raise your thinking above your involuntary impulses. By no means do you need to give up all of your spontaneous impulses and selfish desires in order to achieve. Some of these, however, must be sacrificed. If you always act on your impulses, you won't be able to plan or reflect before you react. You won't find or develop your hidden talents, and you'll fail in every endeavor. If you haven't begun to consciously control your thoughts, you aren't in a position to be in charge of your affairs and take on serious responsibilities. You're not fit to act independently and stand alone.

There can be no progress or achievement without directed action. Your worldly success will be determined by your prudent handling of your natural impulses and the strength of your resolve toward achieving your goals. The more you focus on your purpose and positive thinking, the stronger your character will become, and the greater and more lasting your success will be. You're only limited by your thoughts, which you alone choose.

The universe doesn't reward greedy, dishonest, or mean people, even though it may appear to do so at times. The universe helps honest, compassionate, positive people. All of history's great teachers have said as much in varying ways. To test the truth of this, you simply have to persist in thinking positively and thereby strengthen your character.

Every kind of achievement is the end result of effort and positive thinking. Intellectual accomplishments are the result of people dedicating their thoughts to the search for knowledge, and focusing on discovering beauty and truth in life and nature. While these pursuits are sometimes linked to vanity and ambition, success isn't the outcome of those characteristics—it's the natural result of long and arduous efforts and of hopeful and unselfish thoughts. Spiritual achievements are the end result of holy desires. A person who constantly ponders noble and lofty ideals, focusing on everything that's right and generous, will become wise and noble in character and will rise into a position of influence and reverence.

You may achieve great success and strengthen your character only to later descend into weakness and unhappiness by engaging in negative thinking. The success you attain by thinking positively can only be maintained through vigilant monitoring of the quality of your thoughts. Many people let their defenses down when success seems assured, only to rapidly fall back into failure.

All achievements, whether in the business, intellectual, or spiritual world, are the result of consciously directed thought and are governed by the same law. The only difference lies in what is attained.

Remember: If you sacrifice only a little, you'll accomplish only a little; if you sacrifice a lot, you'll achieve a lot. If you sacrifice even more, you'll attain great things.

Chapter Six

MAKING YOUR DREAMS
YOUR REALITY

Dreamers are the world's saviors. Even as we experience trials and engage in pessimism, we're nourished by the magnificent visions of dreamers. We can't forget them, and we can't allow their teachings to fade away and die. Composers, sculptors, painters, poets, prophets, and sages are the architects of our ideals. Our world is beautiful because of them, and without them, the general populace would perish.

Whoever nurtures a beautiful vision or a grand ideal in his or her heart will one day make it reality. Columbus dreamed of another world, and he discovered it. Copernicus envisioned a multiplicity of worlds and a wider universe, and he revealed it. Buddha conceived of a spiritual world of flawless perfection and peace, and he entered into it.

Hold your visions and ideals dear to your heart. Cherish the music that stirs in your heart and the beauty that forms in your mind, for out of them magnificence will emerge. Stay true to your dreams, and eventually your world will be built around them. Simply ask and you'll receive!

To desire is to obtain, and to aspire to is to achieve. Natural law doesn't allow your basest desires to thrive and your purest aspirations to starve. Dream magnificent dreams, and as you dream, so you will become. Your visions and ideals are the promise of what you'll create someday. Every great achievement was at one time just a fantasy. The oak sleeps in the acorn, the bird waits in the egg, and a glorious soul stirs in you. Your dreams are the seeds of your reality.

You may not like the current condition of your life, but it will quickly change if you strive to achieve your ideals. You simply can't grow within and stand still without. Imagine a young person worn down by poverty and hard labor. She works long hours in a factory and hasn't been taught to read or write. She dreams of better things—of learning, intelligence, beauty, and a life of ease. This vision of a more fulfilling existence empowers her and drives her to action. She focuses her free time and limited resources on the development of her hidden powers. In a short time, she has so altered her character through positive thinking that she can no longer work in the factory. This menial work clashes with her new mentality, and with the ease of throwing a coat aside, she leaves it behind forever as new doors open that harmonize with her expanding consciousness.

Years later, this same woman is now the master of her mind's forces. She wields her thoughts with great influence and power. She speaks, and lives are changed. Men and women hang upon her words and remold their characters. Like a sun, she becomes the fixed and luminous center around which the lives of many people evolve. She has turned her youthful dream into reality—she has become one with her ideal.

You'll also realize the vision of your heart, be it humble or beautiful or a mixture of both. You'll always gravitate toward that which you love the most, even if it's kept secret. Your life will be the exact result of your thoughts, and you'll receive what you earn—no more and no less. Whatever your present conditions may be, you'll fall, remain, or rise in accordance with your thoughts, visions, and ideals. You'll become as small as your most primitive desire and as great as your most grand hope. Eventually you'll walk through doors that have always seemed closed to you. You'll enter the office of your mentor and he will say, "I have nothing more to teach you." You will have become the master of your thoughts, who so recently dreamed the great vision that is now your life.

Unthinking, ignorant, lazy people who only see the apparent effects of things and not their causes talk of luck, fortune, and chance. When they notice a man grow rich, they say, "He's so lucky!" When they see a woman succeed intellectually, they grumble, "Someone must have pulled some strings for her." When they notice the wide influence of others, they remark, "They always get the breaks." They don't see all the trials, failures, and struggles that these folks have voluntarily come up against to gain their experience. They have no knowledge of the sacrifices these successful people have made. They're unaware of the enormous effort exerted and faith exercised by those who overcome apparently insurmountable obstacles in order to realize the visions of their hearts. They don't know the darkness and heart-aches, seeing only the light and joy, and they call this "luck." They don't see the long and arduous journeys, seeing only the achievement, and they call this "good fortune." They don't understand the law of thought but only perceive the result, calling it "chance."

In all human affairs, there are efforts and there are results. The amount of effort is the measure of the result; chance isn't. All your gifts, powers; and intellectual, material, and spiritual possessions are the fruits of your hard work—of your focused thoughts that transform your dreams into your reality. Your life is built on the visions that you paint in your mind and the ideals you hold dear in your heart. This you will become.

Chapter Seven

HOW TO DEVELOP
A CALM MIND

A calm mind is one of the beautiful jewels of wisdom. It results from the patient and long exertion of self-control, and its materialization reflects great experience and deep understanding of the laws and operations of thought.

People gain serenity in direct proportion to their acceptance of the fact that they're the result of their thoughts. A calm mind also necessitates the recognition that other people are the result of their thoughts. Through this knowledge, you can see more and more clearly how conditions are the result of cause and effect. Knowing this, you stop fussing, fuming, worrying, and grieving; and instead, you remain poised, steadfast, and serene.

Calm people, having learned how to govern themselves, know how to lead others. Others, in turn, revere the spiritual strength of serene people and feel that they can learn from them and rely upon them. The more tranquil you become, the more you'll succeed. For example, small business owners will find that their bottom lines increase as they develop greater self-control and composure, because people always prefer to deal with someone who has an even demeanor.

Strong, calm people are always loved and admired; they're like shade-giving trees in arid areas or sheltering rocks in a storm. Who doesn't prefer to be in the presence of a person who's sweet tempered and lives a balanced life? For calm people, it doesn't matter whether it rains or shines or what comes their way, because they're always kind, gentle, and coolheaded. That exquisite poise of character that we call serenity is the last lesson we learn. It's more precious than wisdom and more desirable than wealth—in fact, money becomes insignificant in comparison to a peaceful life.

A calm soul no longer rides a roller coaster of ever-changing emotions or reacts hastily to whatever comes his or her way. Yet how many people do you know who poison their lives with their explosive tempers? Who destroy every beautiful moment? Who embarrass themselves by feeding on drama? Who allow themselves to be overcome by anxiety, doubt, or grief? The great majority of people ruin their lives and create unhappiness because of a lack of self-control. We meet very few people who are well balanced and possess the exquisite poise of restraint.

Serenity is the reflection of a person who has fully realized his or her dreams and ideals. Peaceful people's thoughts are controlled and positive, allowing them to tame the storms around them. Tempest-tossed souls can take heart in knowing that regardless of their circumstances, they have the power to create such calm in their own lives.

Monitor your thoughts with vigilance, nurturing positive thinking and guarding against negativity. The master is within you! Take charge of your thoughts and you'll be in the driver's seat of your life. Self-control brings you strength, and calmness is power. If you've trained your mind that your word is law, you only need to say to your heart and your mind, "Peace," and you'll become still.

PART II

How to Change Your Thinking

THE KEY EXPERIENTIAL PROCESS

Change in your life requires change in your thinking. Many people have found the exercises in this part of the book useful in learning to think more positively on an ongoing basis. We recommend completing them sequentially. You can then return to a given exercise whenever you find yourself facing a related issue. An audio version of The Key Experiential Process activity is on the CD that accompanies this book.

The importance of this simple exercise can't be overstated; it's well worth your undivided attention, so please save it for a time when you can make it your sole focus. (We don't recommend that you try to do this while driving or multitasking in any other way.) The CD is also well worth repeated listenings, as many people have told us that the second or third time was as useful as the first.

Part of the power of this process comes from its elegant simplicity, and it works best when you follow the instructions as precisely as possible.

This first process is called "The Key" because it opens the gateway to the power of the seven additional transformational activities, which correspond to each chapter of *As a Man Thinketh*, which follow. It's also the experiential process that opened the gateway for a generation of teachers, such as Neale Donald Walsch (the author of *Conversations with God).*

Step one: Seat yourself comfortably in a quiet place where you're unlikely to be interrupted for the next 10 to 15 minutes. Take a few moments to relax and get into a receptive mood.

Step two: Direct your attention to the thoughts that are passing through your mind. Notice that you don't have to force your thoughts to flow—they come on their own without any conscious doing on your part. Now consider this: With the smallest effort, you can change your thinking. And by simply making some minor adjustments in the way your mind works, you'll also begin to effect positive changes in the outer circumstances of your life.

Step three: Begin to notice two different kinds of thoughts. (There are many different kinds of thoughts, but for now, let's focus on just these two.) One kind is the spontaneous thought that just pops up in your mind. The second is the type of thought that you initiate consciously.

For the purpose of this exercise, focus on thinking in words, rather than pictures or memories. Use apples as an example. When you saw or heard "apples," you might have pictured fruit in your mind. Perhaps your apples were green or red or some other color. Right now, try to think about apples without pictures, but with words. Think, *I like apples.* Repeat that thought a few times: *I like apples.* (If you don't like apples, then think, *I don't like apples.*)

Keep replaying the thought more and more faintly until you're not actually hearing the words in your mind, but you know you're still thinking them. You're saying the sentence as a very faint thought.

Step four: Now you'll learn how you can change negative thoughts to positive ones in that same effortless way. Use as an example a thought that many of us have had: *I have to go to the dentist.* Let's say you wake up one day realizing that you have a dental appointment on your calendar. The thought *I have to go to the dentist* automatically appears in your mind.

Think this several times in your mind, very quietly: *I have to go to the dentist.* Linguists say that the word *have* in this context implies a sense of burden, that it's something it's better not to do. Psycholinguists tell us that when we use *have* in this context, we disempower ourselves by implying that we're merely the victims of what we must do. Whether or not you agree with these experts, go ahead and experiment with changing this thought in the following way:

Think, *I have to go to the dentist,* then after a few repetitions, change the sentence to: *I plan to go to the dentist.* Repeat the new sentence a number of times, noticing whether you feel a subtle difference in your mind and body.

After you've done that, make another change to the sentence. Begin by repeating the thought, *I have to go to the dentist*. This time, change the thought to: *I choose to go to the dentist*. Think that over and over. Notice differences in your mind and body as you claim this more empowering thought.

Now go to a very positive thought about the same subject. Try out the following sentence in your mind: *I appreciate the benefits of dentistry*. Say it a few times quietly in your mind.

See if you notice the subtle difference in your mind and body when you contrast *I have to go to the dentist* with *I appreciate the benefits of dentistry*.

Step five: Now apply what you've learned to a thought of your own selection. Take a moment now to think of a negative or limiting thought you've noticed in your life. Here are some that people have mentioned:

- I'm afraid of public speaking.
- I can't ever find the time to exercise.
- I can't seem to lose weight.

- I don't like parties.
- It's hard to meet interesting men/women.

Pick a negative or limiting thought from your own life and express it in one sentence. Say it quietly in your mind a few times, noticing how it feels in your mind and body.

Now choose a positive, empowering thought about the same issue. For example, if you've been saying *I'm afraid of public speaking,* make up a sentence like *I enjoy speaking in public.* If that feels like too much of a jump, you could say, *I'd like to learn how to enjoy speaking in public.* The exact sentence you use is up to you, just as long as it has a positive quality.

Now, quietly in your mind, repeat your negative, limiting thought several times. Then, just as quietly, replace it with your positive, empowering one. Repeat the new thought over and over, letting it become more and more subtle and effortless.

Step six: This is how to change your thoughts: Going forward over the next days and weeks, do your best to spot as many negative or limiting thoughts as you possibly can. When you identify them, introduce a new positive affirmation into your thought stream. Just drop in this empowering way of thinking effortlessly, as if it's always been there.

Gradually, with time and practice, your thoughts naturally begin to gravitate in a more empowering and positive direction. In the beginning, though, all you need to remember is to take it one thought at a time. Change one, and before you know it, you'll see positive results in the outer circumstances of your life.

SEVEN ADDITIONAL TRANSFORMATIONAL ACTIVITIES BASED ON *AS A MAN THINKETH*

Activity 1: Drifts to Shifts

To think positively on a regular basis, you need to monitor your thoughts and consciously choose to shift from negative thought patterns to positive ones. A powerful way to achieve this is to identify your "drifts," such as complaining or blaming, and determine effective "shifts," such as appreciating or taking responsibility.

For example, let's say you often find yourself complaining about the company you work for. This thought pattern only serves to increase the negativity surrounding your job. Instead, you can choose to consciously shift from complaining to appreciation, opting to review in your mind what you appreciate about the work you do—including your salary! Or you can shift to positive visualization by imagining your ideal job.

Make a list of your common drifts in the left column of the following chart. Then make a list of effective shifts next to those drifts in the right column that can shift you from negative to positive thinking. We've started you off with an example.

[You might need to use additional paper for some of these activities.]

COMMON DRIFTS	EFFECTIVE SHIFTS
Complaining	Appreciating

Over the next week, pay attention to your thoughts. When you notice them drifting into negative patterns, consciously choose to shift to more positive thoughts and actions.

Deepen the Learning

After the end of the week, write down any effects you experienced as a result of this exercise in the space provided below:

_____

_____

_____

_____

∞◇∞

Activity 2: Unlocking Your Conscious Commitment

The concept that your thoughts shape your life can be a difficult one to accept. This is especially true when you believe that you're focusing energy on a positive result but find yourself continually producing a negative outcome. This unwanted outcome occurs due to your unconscious generation of pessimistic thoughts about the same issue.

For example, imagine that you're single but want to be married. You've tried everything in the book—Internet dating, therapy, asking people out, waiting to be asked out—to no avail. You remain single because at your core you're unconsciously more committed to being single than being married. To achieve your desired outcome, you need to unlock that unconscious commitment to the negative result.

To identify your unconscious commitment, try the following exercise: In the space below, write the positive result you desire. (For example, "I want to be married.")

Positive result:_____

Now write out the negative outcome you've been creating. (Using the above example, it might be "I never seriously date anyone.")

Negative outcome: _____

Ask yourself the following series of five "Why?" questions, always writing down the first thought that comes to your mind:

Why am I creating this negative outcome? (Using the marriage example, you could say, "I'm afraid of rejection.")

_____

_____

Now, referring to the answer you just gave, ask yourself why a second time. (In other words, "Why am I afraid of rejection? Because if I'm rejected, it might mean that I'm not lovable.")

_____

_____

Look back to your second answer and ask yourself why a third time. ("Why does it mean I'm not lovable if someone rejects me?")

_____

_____

Ask yourself why a fourth time with respect to the answer directly above. (You get the idea.)

_____

_____

Read your fourth answer, and concerning that response, ask yourself why one final time.

_____

_____

Accept your truths about your unconscious commitment by taking a deep breath and stating them out loud: *"I am unconsciously committed to* [state the negative result you keep producing] *because . . ."* [state each of your answers to the five *why* questions].

Now change your unconscious commitment by writing down a conscious commitment to whatever you truly want to create and are willing to work toward whole-heartedly:

I commit to:

_____

_____

Say this conscious commitment out loud, moving or dancing if desired, until your whole body feels in harmony with it.

Deepen the Learning

Each morning this week, take a minute when you wake up to say your conscious commitment out loud. Repeat this statement until your whole body resonates with your goal.

Activity 3: Lifestream Breathing

Your thoughts have a direct impact on your health. Every time you insert a positive thought into a negative thought stream, you're moving away from disease and toward health.

In addition to regularly generating positive thoughts, you can improve your health by letting positive energy flow through your body and mind. You can do all this simply by breathing more deeply. To further awaken the vibrant energy residing within you, we invite you to try a special technique called Lifestream Breathing.

We've noticed that most people breathe while holding their backs stiff and their abdomens tight. This stiffness and tightness keeps your diaphragm from moving through its full range of motion, forcing you to inhale into your chest and preventing you from ever taking a full breath. To counteract this, when doing Lifestream Breathing, you move your spine and relax and expand your belly as you breathe. This change in technique creates such dramatic physical results that after just a few breaths you'll feel more alive and energized and also feel more centered and at ease.

Here's how it works: Sit toward the front of a chair with your feet comfortably planted on the floor and your hands on your thighs. Gently and slowly arch and round the small of your back. This motion will cause you to rock forward and back and move your pelvis all the way forward and back. (If you're familiar with yoga, this is like switching between cat and dog positions while being seated.) Take six to seven seconds to arch your back and six to seven seconds to round it.

As you arch the small of your back, tilt your chin up toward the ceiling. As you round the small of your back, tilt your chin down toward the floor.

Now add breathing to the movement. Breathe all the way into your relaxed belly as you arch the small of your back and look up. Breathe all the way out as you round the small of your back and look down. Continue with Lifestream Breathing until you feel a powerful flow of ease throughout your body.

Deepen the Learning

We recommend breathing this way for ten minutes each morning to achieve optimal health, stress release, and vibrancy. (More information on these and other activities related to breathing can be found at **www.hendricks.com.**)

Activity 4: Living Purposefully

By adding direction to your thoughts, you can quickly achieve everything you desire—from banishing addictions to attracting genuine love to coming up with the next great invention. The most powerful purpose you can focus on is the unique objective of your individual life. When you know your life's purpose, you have an anchor that stabilizes you. You can make better decisions by simply asking if a given action supports or detracts from your goal. This central goal, however, isn't always immediately clear to each of us.

To discover your unique purpose, I invite you to spend time breathing deeply and sitting quietly as you focus on your ambition—or, if you prefer, get up and move around in whatever way makes you smile! Take time to notice any thoughts that bubble up in your mind. Be patient and enjoy the journey of discovery—even if it's a longer path than you prefer to follow.

If you're still having a difficult time identifying your purpose after a number of attempts, complete the following activity to help move your mind toward the answer.

- Write down all the things you loved to do as a child—no editing!

_____

_____

_____

_____

- List the activities you love doing now—the things you get lost in when time just flies by.

_____

_____

_____

_____

_____

Answer the following questions, writing down the first thought that comes to your mind:

- **What did you dream of doing when you were a child?**

_____

_____

- **What unique talent do you bring to the world?**

_____

_____

- **What special gift do you offer others?**

_____

_____

- If you had a magic lamp to make the world a better place, what would you ask for?

- What could you do every day and enjoy it so much that you'd never want to retire?

- What could you say on your deathbed that would show that your life was a success?

- **What is your life's purpose right now?**

_____

_____

Keep meditating on your ambitions, returning to these questions until your unique goal is clear. Then, write it down.

- **My life's purpose is:**

_____

_____

Deepen the Learning
Now that you've identified your life's purpose, make a commitment to doing something that will let you live out that mission more fully each day.

Activity 5: Successful Positive Thinking

Your successes and failures are the direct result of your own thoughts. As such, you need to be sure to think of what you want in clear, positive terminology instead of negative terms.

For example, if you want to lose ten pounds, you'll support your goal by thinking, *I'm losing ten pounds. I'm thin.* You'll sabotage your weight loss if your thought is simply, *I want to lose ten pounds.* The energy you generate will be around wanting instead of achieving. You'll also risk staying overweight if you just think, *I don't want to be fat anymore.* Even though it's often easier to identify what you *don't* want than what you do, the universal energy within you and around you often fails to hear the "not" and just delivers the primary thought—in this case, being fat!

You can more quickly achieve your goals by vigilantly monitoring your thoughts and replacing any negative thoughts with positive, active ones. Instead of focusing on what you *don't* want, identify exactly what you *do*

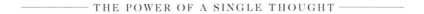

want and then think of this goal as if you're already on the way to achieving it. Here's a helpful activity to get you on track.

Make a list of what you don't want in your life anymore, and then turn each item into a positive statement of what you do want.

What I Don't Want	What I Do Want

Now turn each of your statements in the "What I Do Want" column into clear action phrases, using the present tense:

_____

_____

_____

_____

_____

Deepen the Learning

Now that you know what you want, visualize each thing on your list, adding as much vivid detail as possible. Think of what you want, using your positive phrases and visualizations whenever associated thoughts enter your mind.

Trust yourself and the universe to deliver exactly what you want!

Activity 6: Outrageous Desires

If you want to make your dreams your reality, you first need to start dreaming! Set aside the more rational side of your brain and the voice that says, "I can't do that." Grab a pen and immediately start writing a list of the most outrageous things you'd do or create if nothing held you back. Write down everything that comes to mind—no editing!

My Most Outrageous Desires

_____

_____

_____

_____

_____

Just by making this list, you've put the wheels in motion for achieving everything you desire. Watch in wonder as you notice people and the world around you supporting your dreams.

Deepen the Learning

Go back to your list and choose one dream that you would like to accomplish now. Take five to ten minutes to visualize this dream in all its glory. What does it look like? What are you wearing? Who's with you? What are you feeling? What other details can you imagine?

Now make a list of the steps you need to accomplish in order to turn your dream into your reality. Take time to research these steps if necessary. Then watch your dream come true!!

◇⬦◇

Activity 7: A Seven-Minute Calming and Manifestation Process

Calming your mind can take many years of practice and commitment. You can begin by setting your intentions for each day using the following meditation. By taking a few minutes each morning to focus your actions, you'll feel more centered, and you'll be able to turn your dreams into reality more quickly.

Breathing deeply, spend one minute with each of these processes:

- Connect with your spirit in any way that feels comfortable to you. You might feel it in your body, or visualize a spiritual image in your mind.

- State your life's purpose as you know it right now, and revel in its power. In your mind, say, "The purpose of my life is _____."

- Visualize successfully completing your major projects.

- Review what you want to accomplish today.

- Appreciate what has happened in the last 24 hours.

- Listen silently to the wisdom of the universe.

- Return to yourself and reconnect with your soul.

PART III

THE ORIGINAL VERSION OF *AS A MAN THINKETH*

Here's the original version of *As a Man Thinketh,* written by James Allen in the Victorian language of his time. We've included this older version so that curious readers can compare our modernized version with Mr. Allen's original. We hope you approve of our revisions, and we also welcome your comments, questions, and feedback with respect to our interpretation.

Chapter One

THOUGHT AND CHARACTER

The aphorism "As a man thinketh in his heart so is he" not only embraces the whole of a man's being, but is so comprehensive as to reach out to every condition and circumstance of his life. A man is literally what he thinks, his character being the complete sum of all his thoughts.

As the plant springs from, and could not be without, the seed, so every act of a man springs from the hidden seeds of thought, and could not have appeared without them. This applies equally to those acts called "spontaneous" and "unpremeditated" as to those which are deliberately executed.

Act is the blossom of thought, and joy and suffering are its fruits; thus does a man garner in the sweet and bitter fruitage of his own husbandry.

Thought in the mind hath made us
    what we are by thought we wrought and built.
    If a man's mind
    hath evil thoughts, pain comes on him
    as comes the wheel the ox behind . . .
If one endure
    in purity of thought, joy follows him
As his own shadow—sure.

Man is a growth by law, and not a creation by arti-fice, and cause and effect is as absolute and undeviating in the hidden realm of thought as in the world of vis-ible and material things. A noble and godlike character is not a thing of favor or chance, but is the natural result of continued effort in right thinking, the effect of long-cherished association with godlike thoughts. An ignoble and bestial character, by the same process, is the result of the continued harboring of groveling thoughts.

Man is made or unmade by himself; in the armory of thought he forges the weapons by which he destroys himself. He also fashions the tools with which he builds for himself heavenly mansions of joy and strength and peace. By the right choice and true application of thought, man ascends to the Divine Perfection; by the abuse and wrong application of thought, he descends below the level of the beast. Between these two extremes are all the grades of character, and man is their maker and master.

Of all the beautiful truths pertaining to the soul which have been restored and brought to light in this age, none is more gladdening or fruitful of divine promise and confidence than this—that man is the master of thought, the molder of character, and maker and shaper of condition, environment, and destiny.

As a being of Power, Intelligence, and Love, and the lord of his own thoughts, man holds the key to every situation, and contains within himself that transforming and regenerative agency by which he may make himself what he wills.

Man is always the master, even in his weakest and most abandoned state; but in his weakness and degradation he is the foolish master who misgoverns his "household." When he begins to reflect upon his condition, and to search diligently for the Law upon which his being is established, he then becomes the wise master, directing his energies with intelligence, and fashioning his thoughts to fruitful issues. Such is the conscious master, and man can only thus become by discovering within himself the laws of thought; which discovery is totally a matter of application, self-analysis, and experience.

Only by much searching and mining are gold and diamonds obtained, and man can find every truth connected with his being if he will dig deep into the mine of his soul. And that he is the maker of his character, the molder of his life, and the builder of his destiny, he may unerringly prove: if he will watch, control, and alter his thoughts, tracing their effects upon himself, upon others, and upon his life and circumstances; if he will link cause and effect by patient practice and investigation, utilizing his every experience, even to the most trivial, as a means of obtaining that knowledge of himself. In this direction, as in no other, is the law absolute that "He that seeketh findeth; and to him that knocketh it shall be opened"; for only by patience, practice, and ceaseless importunity can a man enter the Door of the Temple of Knowledge.

Chapter Two

EFFECT OF THOUGHT
ON CIRCUMSTANCE

A man's mind may be likened to a garden, which may be intelligently cultivated or allowed to run wild; but whether cultivated or neglected, it must, and will, bring forth. If no useful seeds are put into it, then an abundance of useless weed seeds will fall therein, and will continue to produce their kind.

Just as a gardener cultivates his plot, keeping it free from weeds, and growing the flowers and fruits which he requires, so may a man tend the garden of his mind, weeding out all the wrong, useless, and impure thoughts, and cultivating toward perfection the flowers and fruits of right, useful, and pure thoughts. By pursuing this process, a man sooner or later discovers that he is the master gardener of his soul, the director of his life. He also reveals, within himself, the laws of thought, and understands with ever-increasing accuracy, how the thought forces and mind elements operate in the shaping of his character, circumstances, and destiny.

Thought and character are one, and as character can only manifest and discover itself through environment and circumstance, the outer conditions of a person's life will always be found to be harmoniously related to his inner state. This does not mean that a man's circumstances at any given time are an indication of his entire character, but that those circumstances are so intimately connected with some vital thought element within himself that, for the time being, they are indispensable to his development.

Every man is where he is by the law of his being. The thoughts which he has built into his character have brought him there, and in the arrangement of his life there is no element of chance, but all is the result of a law which cannot err. This is just as true of those who feel "out of harmony" with their surroundings as of those who are contented with them.

As the progressive and evolving being, man is where he is that he may learn and that he may grow; and as he learns the spiritual lesson which any circumstance contains for him, it passes away and gives place to other circumstances.

Man is buffeted by circumstances so long as he believes himself to be the creature of outside conditions. But when he realizes that he may command the hidden soil and seeds of his being out of which circumstances grow, he then becomes the rightful master of himself.

That circumstances grow out of thought every man knows who has for any length of time practiced self-control and self-purification, for he will have noticed that the alteration in his circumstances has been in exact ratio with his altered mental condition. So true is this that when a man earnestly applies himself to remedy the defects in his character, and makes swift and marked progress, he passes rapidly through a succession of vicissitudes.

The soul attracts that which it secretly harbors; that which it loves, and also that which it fears. It reaches the height of its cherished aspirations. It falls to the level of its unchastened desires—and circumstances are the means by which the soul receives its own.

Every thought seed sown or allowed to fall into the mind, and to take root there, produces its own, blossoming sooner or later into act, and bearing its own fruitage of opportunity and circumstance. Good thoughts bear good fruit, bad thoughts bad fruit.

The outer world of circumstance shapes itself to the inner world of thought, and both pleasant and unpleasant external conditions are factors which make for the ultimate good of the individual. As the reaper of his own harvest, man learns both by suffering and bliss.

A man does not come to the almshouse or the jail by the tyranny of fate or circumstance, but by the pathway of groveling thoughts and base desires. Nor does a pure-minded man fall suddenly into crime by stress of any mere external force; the criminal thought had long been secretly fostered in the heart, and the hour of opportunity revealed its gathered power.

Circumstance does not make the man; it reveals him to himself. No such conditions can exist as descending into vice and its attendant sufferings apart from vicious inclinations, or ascending into virtue and its pure happiness without the continued cultivation of virtuous aspirations. And man, therefore, as the Lord and master of thought, is the maker of himself, the shaper and author of environment. Even at birth the soul comes to its own, and through every step of its earthly pilgrimage it attracts those combinations of conditions which reveal itself, which are the reflections of its own purity and impurity, its strength and weakness.

Men do not attract that which they want, but that which they are. Their whims, fancies, and ambitions are thwarted at every step, but their inmost thoughts and desires are fed with their own food, be it foul or clean. The "divinity that shapes our ends" is in ourselves; it is our very self. Man is manacled only by himself. Thought and action are the jailers of Fate—they imprison, being base. They are also the angels of Freedom—they liberate, being noble. Not what he wishes and prays for does a man get, but what he justly earns. His wishes and prayers are only gratified and answered when they harmonize with his thoughts and actions.

In the light of this truth, what, then, is the meaning of "fighting against circumstances"? It means that a man is continually revolting against an effect without, while all the time he is nourishing and preserving its cause in his heart. That cause may take the form of a conscious vice or an unconscious weakness; but whatever it is, it stubbornly retards the efforts of its possessor, and thus calls aloud for remedy.

Men are anxious to improve their circumstances, but are unwilling to improve themselves. They therefore remain bound. The man who does not shrink from self-crucifixion can never fail to accomplish the object upon which his heart is set. This is as true of earthly as of heavenly things. Even the man whose sole object is to acquire wealth must be prepared to make great personal sacrifices before he can accomplish his object; and how much more so he who would realize a strong and well-poised life?

Here is a man who is wretchedly poor. He is extremely anxious that his surroundings and home comforts should be improved. Yet all the time he shirks his work, and considers he is justified in trying to deceive his employer on the ground of the insufficiency of his wages. Such a man does not understand the simplest rudiments of those principles which are the basis of true prosperity. He is not only totally unfitted to rise out of his wretchedness, but is actually attracting to himself a still deeper wretchedness by dwelling in, and acting out, indolent, deceptive, and unmanly thoughts.

Here is a rich man who is the victim of a painful and persistent disease as the result of gluttony. He is willing to give large sums of money to get rid of it, but he will not sacrifice his gluttonous desires. He wants to gratify his taste for rich and unnatural foods and have his health as well. Such a man is totally unfit to have health, because he has not yet learned the first principles of a healthy life.

Here is an employer of labor who adopts crooked measures to avoid paying the regulation wage, and, in the hope of making larger profits, reduces the wages of his workpeople. Such a man is altogether unfitted for prosperity. And when he finds himself bankrupt, both as regards reputation and riches, he blames circumstances, not knowing that he is the sole author of his condition.

I have introduced these three cases merely as illustrative of the truth that man is the cause (though nearly always unconsciously) of his circumstances. That, while aiming at the good end, he is continually frustrating its accomplishment by encouraging thoughts and desires which cannot possibly harmonize with that end. Such cases could be multiplied and varied almost indefinitely, but this is not necessary. The reader can, if he so resolves, trace the action of the laws of thought in his own mind and life, and until this is done, mere external facts cannot serve as a ground of reasoning.

Circumstances, however, are so complicated, thought is so deeply rooted, and the conditions of happiness vary so vastly with individuals, that a man's entire soul condition (although it may be known to himself) cannot be judged by another from the external aspect of his life alone.

A man may be honest in certain directions, yet suffer privations. A man may be dishonest in certain directions, yet acquire wealth. But the conclusion usually formed that the one man fails because of his particular honesty, and that the other prospers because of his particular dishonesty, is the result of a superficial judgment, which assumes that the dishonest man is almost totally corrupt, and honest man almost entirely virtuous. In the light of a deeper knowledge and wider experience, such judgment is found to be erroneous. The dishonest man may have some admirable virtues which the other does not possess; and the honest man obnoxious vices which are absent in the other. The honest man reaps the good results of his honest thoughts and acts; he also brings upon himself the sufferings which his vices produce. The dishonest man likewise garners his own suffering and happiness.

It is pleasing to human vanity to believe that one suffers because of one's virtue. But not until a man has extirpated every sickly, bitter, and impure thought from his mind, and washed every sinful stain from his soul, can he be in a position to know and declare that his sufferings are the result of his good, and not of his bad qualities.

And on the way to that supreme perfection, he will have found working in his mind and life, the Great Law which is absolutely just, and which cannot give good for evil, evil for good. Possessed of such knowledge, he will then know, looking back upon his past ignorance and blindness, that his life is, and always was, justly ordered, and that all his past experiences, good and bad, were the equitable outworking of his evolving, yet unevolved self.

Good thoughts and actions can never produce bad results. Bad thoughts and actions can never produce good results. This is but saying that nothing can come from corn but corn, nothing from nettles but nettles. Men understand this law in the natural world, and work with it. But few understand it in the mental and moral world (though its operation there is just as simple and undeviating), and they, therefore, do not cooperate with it.

Suffering is always the effect of wrong thought in some direction. It is an indication that the individual is out of harmony with himself, with the Law of his being. The sole and supreme use of suffering is to purify, to burn out all that is useless and impure. Suffering ceases for him who is pure. There could be not object in burning gold after the dross had been removed, and a perfectly pure and enlightened being could not suffer.

The circumstances which a man encounters with suffering are the result of his own mental inharmony. The circumstances which a man encounters with blessedness, not material possessions, is the measure of right thought. Wretchedness, not lack of material possessions, is the measure of wrong thought. A man may be cursed and rich; he may be blessed and poor. Blessedness and riches are only joined together when the riches are rightly and wisely used. And the poor man only descends into wretchedness when he regards his lot as a burden unjustly imposed.

Indigence and indulgence are the two extremes of wretchedness. They are both equally unnatural and the result of mental disorder. A man is not rightly conditioned until he is a happy, healthy, and prosperous being. And happiness, health, and prosperity are the result of a harmonious adjustment of the inner with the outer, of the man with his surroundings.

A man only begins to be a man when he ceases to whine and revile, and commences to search for the hidden justice which regulates his life. And as he adapts his mind to that regulating factor, he ceases to accuse others as the cause of his condition, and builds himself up in strong and noble thoughts. He ceases to kick against circumstances, but begins to use them as aids to his more rapid progress, and as a means of discovering the hidden powers and possibilities within himself.

Law, not confusion, is the dominating principle in the universe. Justice, not injustice, is the soul and substance of life. And righteousness, not corruption, is the molding and moving force in the spiritual government of the world. This being so, man has but to right himself to find that the universe is right; and during the process of putting himself right, he will find that as he alters his thoughts toward things and other people, things and other people will alter toward him.

The proof of this truth is in every person, and it therefore admits of easy investigation by systematic introspection and self-analysis. Let a man radically alter his thoughts, and he will be astonished at the rapid transformation it will effect in the material conditions of his life.

Men imagine that thought can be kept secret, but it cannot. It rapidly crystallizes into habit, and habit solidifies into habits of drunkenness and sensuality, which solidify into circumstances of destitution and disease. Impure thoughts of every kind crystallize into enervating and confusing habits, which solidify into distracting and adverse circumstances. Thoughts of fear, doubt, and indecision crystallize into weak, unmanly, and irresolute habits, which solidify into circumstances of failure, indigence, and slavish dependence.

Lazy thoughts crystallize into habits of uncleanliness and dishonesty, which solidify into circumstances of foulness and beggary. Hateful and condemnatory thoughts crystallize into habits of accusation and violence, which solidify into circumstances of injury and persecution. Selfish thoughts of all kinds crystallize into habits of self-seeking, which solidify into circumstances more or less distressing.

On the other hand, beautiful thoughts of all crystallize into habits of grace and kindliness, which solidify into genial and sunny circumstances. Pure thoughts crystallize into habits of temperance and self-control, which solidify into circumstances of repose and peace. Thoughts of courage, self-reliance, and decision crystallize into manly habits, which solidify into circumstances of success, plenty, and freedom.

Energetic thoughts crystallize into habits of cleanliness and industry, which solidify into circumstances of pleasantness. Gentle and forgiving thoughts crystallize into habits of gentleness, which solidify into protective and preservative circumstances. Loving and unselfish thoughts crystallize into habits of self-forgetfulness for others, which solidify into circumstances of sure and abiding prosperity and true riches.

A particular train of thought persisted in, be it good or bad, cannot fail to produce its results on the character and circumstances. A man cannot directly choose his circumstances, but he can choose his thoughts, and so indirectly, yet surely, shape his circumstances.

Nature helps every man to the gratification of the thoughts which he most encourages, and opportunities are presented which will most speedily bring to the surface both the good and evil thoughts.

Let a man cease from his sinful thoughts, and all the world will soften toward him, and be ready to help him. Let him put away his weakly and sickly thoughts, and lo! opportunities will spring up on every hand to aid his strong resolves. Let him encourage good thoughts, and no hard fate shall bind him down to wretchedness and shame. The world is your kaleidoscope, and the varying combinations of colors which at every succeeding moment it presents to you are the exquisitely adjusted pictures of your ever-moving thoughts.

You will be what you will to be;
Let failure find its false content
In that poor word, "environment,"
But spirit scorns it, and is free.

It masters time, it conquers space;
It cows that boastful trickster, Chance,
And bids the tyrant Circumstance
Uncrown, and fill a servant's place.

The human Will, that force unseen,
The offspring of a deathless Soul,
Can hew a way to any goal,
Though walls of granite intervene.

Be not impatient in delay,
But wait as one who understands;
When spirit rises and commands,
The gods are ready to obey.

Chapter Three

EFFECT OF THOUGHT ON HEALTH AND THE BODY

The body is the servant of the mind. It obeys the operations of the mind, whether they be deliberately chosen or automatically expressed. At the bidding of unlawful thoughts the body sinks rapidly into disease and decay; at the command of glad and beautiful thoughts it becomes clothed with youthfulness and beauty.

Disease and health, like circumstances, are rooted in thought. Sickly thoughts will express themselves through a sickly body. Thoughts of fear have been known to kill a man as speedily as a bullet, and they are continually killing thousands of people just as surely though less rapidly. The people who live in fear of disease are the people who get it. Anxiety quickly demoralizes the whole body, and lays it open to the entrance of disease; while impure thoughts, even if not physically indulged, will soon shatter the nervous system.

Strong, pure, and happy thoughts build up the body in vigor and grace. The body is a delicate and plastic instrument, which responds readily to the thoughts by which it is impressed, and habits of thought will produce their own effects, good or bad, upon it.

Men will continue to have impure and poisoned blood so long as they propagate unclean thoughts. Out of a clean heart comes a clean life and a clean body. Out of a defiled mind proceeds a defiled life and corrupt body. Thought is the fountain of action, life and manifestation; make the fountain pure, and all will be pure.

Change of diet will not help a man who will not change his thoughts. When a man makes his thoughts pure, he no longer desires impure food.

If you would perfect your body, guard your mind. If you would renew your body, beautify your mind. Thoughts of malice, envy, disappointment, and despondency rob the body of its health and grace. A sour face does not come by chance; it is made by sour thoughts. Wrinkles that mar are drawn by folly, passion, pride.

I know a woman of 96 who has the bright, innocent face of a girl. I know a man well under middle age whose face is drawn into inharmonious contours. The one is the result of a sweet and sunny disposition; the other is the outcome of passion and discontent.

As you cannot have a sweet and wholesome abode unless you admit the air and sunshine freely into your rooms, so a strong body and a bright, happy, or serene countenance can only result from the free admittance into the mind of thoughts of joy and good will and serenity.

On the faces of the aged there are wrinkles made by sympathy, others by strong and pure thought, others are carved by passion. Who cannot distinguish them? With those who have lived righteously, age is calm, peaceful, and softly mellowed, like the setting sun. I have recently seen a philosopher on his deathbed. He was not old except in years. He died as sweetly and peacefully as he had lived.

There is no physician like cheerful thought for dissipating the ills of the body; there is no comforter to compare with good will for dispersing the shadows of grief and sorrow. To live continually in thoughts of ill will, cynicism, suspicion, and envy is to be confined in a self-made prison hole. But to think well of all, to be cheerful with all, to patiently learn to find the good in all—such unselfish thoughts are the very portals of heaven; and to dwell day to day in thoughts of peace toward every creature will bring abounding peace to their possessor.

Chapter Four

Thought and Purpose

U ntil thought is linked with purpose there is no intelligent accomplishment. With the majority the bark of thought is allowed to "drift" upon the ocean of life. Aimlessness is a vice, and such drifting must not continue for him who would steer clear of catastrophe and destruction.

They who have no central purpose in their life fall an easy prey to worries, fears, troubles, and self-pityings, all of which are indications of weakness, which lead, just as surely as deliberately planned sins (though by a different route), to failure, unhappiness, and loss, for weakness cannot persist in a power-evolving universe.

A man should conceive of a legitimate purpose in his heart, and set out to accomplish it. He should make this purpose the centralizing point of his thoughts. It may take the form of a spiritual ideal, or it may be a worldly object, according to his nature at the time being. But whichever it is, he should steadily focus his thought forces upon the object which he has set before him. He should make this purpose his supreme duty, and should devote himself to its attainment, not allowing his thoughts to wander away into ephemeral fancies, longings, and imaginings. This is the royal road to self-control and true concentration of thought. Even if he fails again and again to accomplish his purpose (as he necessarily must until weakness is overcome), the strength of character gained will be the measure of his true success, and this will form a new starting point for future power and triumph.

Those who are not prepared for the apprehension of a great purpose, should fix the thoughts upon the faultless performance of their duty, no matter how insignificant their task may appear. Only in this way can the thoughts be gathered and focused, and resolution and energy be developed, which being done, there is nothing which may not be accomplished.

The weakest soul, knowing its own weakness, and believing this truth—that strength can only be developed by effort and practice—will at once begin to exert itself, and adding effort to effort, patience to patience, and strength to strength, will never cease to develop, and will at last grow divinely strong.

As the physically weak man can make himself strong by careful and patient training, so the man of weak thoughts can make them strong by exercising himself in right thinking.

To put away aimlessness and weakness, and to begin to think with purpose, is to enter the ranks of those strong ones who only recognize failure as one of the pathways to attainment; who make all conditions serve them, and who think strongly, attempt fearlessly, and accomplish masterfully.

Having conceived of his purpose, a man should mentally mark out a straight pathway to its achievement, looking neither to the right nor to the left. Doubts and fears should be rigorously excluded; they are disintegrating elements which break up the straight line of effort, rendering it crooked, ineffectual, useless. Thoughts of doubt and fear never accomplish anything, and never can. They always lead to failure. Purpose, energy, power to do, and all strong thoughts cease when doubt and fear creep in.

The will to do springs from the knowledge that we can do. Doubt and fear are the great enemies of knowledge, and he who encourages them, who does not slay them, thwarts himself at every step.

He who has conquered doubt and fear has conquered failure. His every thought is allied with power, and all difficulties are bravely met and wisely overcome. His purposes are seasonably planted, and they bloom and bring forth fruit which does not fall prematurely to the ground.

Thought allied fearlessly to purpose becomes creative force. He who knows this is ready to become something higher and stronger than a mere bundle of wavering thoughts and fluctuating sensations. He who does this has become the conscious and intelligent wielder of his mental powers.

Chapter Five

THE THOUGHT-FACTOR IN ACHIEVEMENT

A ll that a man achieves and all that he fails to achieve is the direct result of his own thoughts. In a justly ordered universe, where loss of equipoise would mean total destruction, individual responsibility must be absolute. A man's weakness and strength, purity and impurity, are his own, and not another man's. They are brought about by himself, and not by another; and they can only be altered by himself, never by another. His condition is also his own, and not another man's. His suffering and his happiness are evolved from within. As he thinks, so he is; as he continues to think, so he remains.

A strong man cannot help a weaker unless the weaker is willing to be helped, and even then the weak man must become strong of himself. He must, by his own efforts, develop the strength which he admires in another. None but himself can alter his condition.

It has been usual for men to think and to say, "Many men are slaves because one is an oppressor; let us hate the oppressor." Now, however, there is among an increasing few a tendency to reverse this judgment, and to say, "One man is an oppressor because many are slaves; let us despise the slaves." The truth is that oppressor and slave are cooperators in ignorance, and, while seeming to afflict each other, are in reality afflicting themselves. A perfect Knowledge perceives the action of law in the weakness of the oppressed and the misapplied power of the oppressor. A perfect Love, seeing the suffering which both states entail, condemns neither. A perfect Compassion embraces both oppressor and oppressed.

He who has conquered weakness, and has put away all selfish thoughts, belongs neither to oppressor nor oppressed. He is free.

A man can only rise, conquer, and achieve by lifting up his thoughts. He can only remain weak, and abject, and miserable by refusing to lift up his thoughts.

Before a man can achieve anything, even in worldly

things, he must lift his thoughts above slavish animal indulgence. He may not, in order to succeed, give up all animality and selfishness, by any means; but a portion of it must, at least, be sacrificed. A man whose first thought is bestial indulgence could neither think clearly nor plan methodically. He could not find and develop his latent resources, and would fail in any undertaking. Not having commenced manfully to control his thoughts, he is not in a position to control affairs and to adopt serious responsibilities. He is not fit to act independently and stand alone, but he is limited only by the thoughts which he chooses.

There can be no progress, no achievement without sacrifice. A man's worldly success will be in the measure that he sacrifices his confused animal thoughts, and fixes his mind on the development of his plans, and the strengthening of his resolution and self-reliance. And the higher he lifts his thoughts, the more manly, upright, and righteous he becomes, the greater will be his success, the more blessed and enduring will be his achievements.

The universe does not favor the greedy, the dishonest, the vicious, although on the mere surface it may sometimes appear to do so; it helps the honest, the magnanimous, the virtuous. All the great Teachers of the ages have declared this in varying forms, and to prove and know it a man has but to persist in making himself more and more virtuous by lifting up his thoughts.

Intellectual achievements are the result of thought consecrated to the search for knowledge, or for the beautiful and true in life and nature. Such achievements may be sometimes connected with vanity and ambition but they are not the outcome of those characteristics. They are the natural outgrowth of long and arduous effort, and of pure and unselfish thoughts.

Spiritual achievements are the consummation of holy aspirations. He who lives constantly in the conception of noble and lofty thoughts, who dwells upon all that is pure and unselfish, will, as surely as the sun reaches its zenith and the moon its full, become wise and noble in character, and rise into a position of influence and blessedness.

Achievement, of whatever kind, is the crown of effort, the diadem of thought. By the aid of self-control, resolution, purity, righteousness, and well-directed thought a man ascends. By the aid of animality, indolence, impurity, corruption, and confusion of thought a man descends.

A man may rise to high success in the world, and even to lofty altitudes in the spiritual realm, and again descend into weakness and wretchedness by allowing arrogant, selfish, and corrupt thoughts to take possession of him.

Victories attained by right thought can only be maintained by watchfulness. Many give way when success is assured, and rapidly fall back into failure.

All achievements, whether in the business, intellectual, or spiritual world, are the result of definitely directed thought, are governed by the same law and are of the same method; the only difference lies in the object of attainment.

He who would accomplish little must sacrifice little. He who would achieve much must sacrifice much. He who would attain highly must sacrifice greatly.

Chapter Six

VISIONS
AND IDEALS

The dreamers are the saviors of the world. As the visible world is sustained by the invisible, so men, through all their trials and sins and sordid vocations, are nourished by the beautiful visions of their solitary dreamers. Humanity cannot forget its dreamers. It cannot let their ideals fade and die. It lives in them. It knows them in the realities which it shall one day see and know.

Composer, sculptor, painter, poet, prophet, sage, these are the makers of the afterworld, the architects of heaven. The world is beautiful because they have lived; without them, laboring humanity would perish.

He who cherishes a beautiful vision, a lofty ideal in his heart, will one day realize it. Columbus cherished a vision of another world, and he discovered it. Copernicus fostered the vision of a multiplicity of worlds and a wider universe, and he revealed it. Buddha beheld the vision of a spiritual world of stainless beauty and perfect peace, and he entered into it.

Cherish your visions. Cherish your ideals. Cherish the music that stirs in your heart, the beauty that forms in your mind, the loveliness that drapes your purest thoughts, for out of them will grow all delightful conditions, all heavenly environment; of these, if you but remain true to them, your world will at last be built.

To desire is to obtain; to aspire is to achieve. Shall man's basest desires receive the fullest measure of gratification, and his purest aspirations starve for lack of sustenance? Such is not the Law. Such a condition of things can never obtain—"Ask and receive."

Dream lofty dreams, and as you dream, so shall you become. Your Vision is the promise of what you shall one day be. Your Ideal is the prophecy of what you shall at last unveil.

The greatest achievement was at first and for a time a dream. The oak sleeps in the acorn; the bird waits in the egg; and in the highest vision of the soul a waking angel stirs. Dreams are the seedlings of realities.

Your circumstances may be uncongenial, but they shall not long remain so if you but perceive an Ideal and strive to reach it. You cannot travel within and stand still without. Here is a youth hard pressed by poverty and labor; confined long hours in an unhealthy workshop; unschooled, and lacking all the arts of refinement. But he dreams of better things. He thinks of intelligence, of refinement, of grace and beauty. He conceives of, mentally builds up, an ideal condition of life. The vision of the wider liberty and a larger scope takes possession of him; unrest urges him to action, and he utilizes all his spare time and means, small though they are, to the development of his latent powers and resources.

Very soon so altered has his mind become that the workshop can no longer hold him. It has become so out of harmony with his mentality that it falls out of his life as a garment is cast aside, and with the growth of opportunities which fit the scope of his expanding powers, he passes out of it forever.

Years later we see this youth as a full-grown man. We find him a master of certain forces of the mind which he wields with worldwide influence and almost unequaled power. In his hands he holds the cords of gigantic responsibilities. He speaks, and lo! lives are changed. Men and women hang upon his words and remold their characters, and, sunlike, he becomes the fixed and luminous center around which innumerable destinies revolve. He has realized the Vision of his youth. He has become one with his Ideal.

And you, too, youthful reader, will realize the Vision (not the idle wish) of your heart, be it base or beautiful, or a mixture of both, for you will always gravitate toward that which you secretly most love. Into your hands will be placed the exact results of your own thoughts; you will receive that which you earn, no more, no less. Whatever your present environment may be, you will fall, remain, or rise with your thoughts, your Vision, your Ideal. You will become as small as your controlling desire; as great as your dominant aspiration.

In the beautiful words of Stanton Kirkham Dave, "You may be keeping accounts, and presently you shall walk out of the door that for so long has seemed to you the barrier of your ideals, and shall find yourself before an audience—the pen still behind your ear, the ink stains on your fingers—and then and there shall pour out the torrent of your inspiration. You may be driving sheep, and you shall wander to the city—bucolic and open mouthed; shall wander under the intrepid guidance of the spirit into the studio of the master, and after a time he shall say, 'I have nothing more to teach you.' And now you have become the master, who did so recently dream of great things while driving sheep. You shall lay down the saw and the plane to take upon yourself the regeneration of the world."

The thoughtless, the ignorant, and the indolent, seeing only the apparent effects of things and not the things themselves, talk of luck, of fortune, and chance. See a man grow rich, they say, "How lucky he is!" Observing another become intellectual, they exclaim, "How highly favored he is!" And noting the saintly character and wide influence of another, they remark, "How chance aids him at every turn!"

They do not see the trials and failures and struggles

which these men have voluntarily encountered in order to gain their experience. They have no knowledge of the sacrifices they have made, of the undaunted efforts they have put forth, of the faith they have exercised, that they might overcome the apparently insurmountable, and realize the Vision of their heart. They do not know the darkness and the heartaches; they only see the light and joy, and call it "luck"; do not see the long and arduous journey, but only behold the pleasant goal, and call it "good fortune"; do not understand the process, but only perceive the result, and call it "chance."

In all human affairs there are efforts, and there are results, and the strength of the effort is the measure of the result. Chance is not. "Gifts," powers, material, intellectual, and spiritual possessions are the fruits of effort. They are thoughts completed, objects accomplished, visions realized.

The vision that you glorify in your mind, the Ideal that you enthrone in your heart—this you will build your life by, this you will become.

Chapter Seven

SERENITY

Calmness of mind is one of the beautiful jewels of wisdom. It is the result of long and patient effort in self-control. Its presence is an indication of ripened experience, and of a more than ordinary knowledge of the laws and operations of thought.

A man becomes calm in the measure that he understands himself as a thought-evolved being, for such knowledge necessitates the understanding of others as the result of thought. As he develops a right understanding, and sees more and more clearly the internal relations of things by the action of cause and effect, he ceases to fuss and fume and worry and grieve, and remains poised, steadfast, serene.

The calm man, having learned how to govern himself, knows how to adapt himself to others; and they, in turn, reverence his spiritual strength, and feel that they can learn of him and rely upon him. The more tranquil a man becomes, the greater is his success, his influence, his power for good. Even the ordinary trader will find his business prosperity increase as he develops a greater self-control and equanimity, for people will always prefer to deal with a man whose demeanor is strongly equable.

The strong calm man is always loved and revered. He is like a shade-giving tree in a thirsty land, or a sheltering rock in a storm. Who does not love a tranquil heart, a sweet-tempered, balanced life? It does not matter whether it rains or shines, or what changes come to those possessing these blessings, for they are always sweet, serene, and calm. That exquisite poise of character which we call serenity is the last lesson culture; it is the flowering of life, the fruitage of the soul. It is precious as wisdom, more to be desired than gold—yea, than even fine gold. How insignificant mere money-seeking looks in comparison with a serene life—a life that dwells in the ocean of Truth, beneath the waves, beyond the reach of tempests, in the Eternal Calm!

How many people we know who sour their lives,

who ruin all that is sweet and beautiful by explosive tempers, who destroy their poise of character, and make bad blood! It is a question whether the great majority of people do not ruin their lives and mar their happiness by lack of self-control. How few people we meet in life who are well-balanced, who have that exquisite poise which is characteristic of the finished character!

Yes, humanity surges with uncontrolled passion, is tumultuous with ungoverned grief, is blown about by anxiety and doubt. Only the wise man, only he whose thoughts are controlled and purified, makes the winds and the storms of the soul obey him.

Tempest-tossed souls, wherever ye may be, under whatsoever conditions ye may live, know this—in the ocean of life the Isles of Blessedness are smiling, and the sunny shore of your ideal awaits your coming. Keep your hand firmly upon the helm of thought. In the bark of your soul reclines the commanding Master; He does but sleep; wake Him. Self-control is strength; Right Thought is mastery; Calmness is power.

Say unto your heart, "Peace, be still!"

ABOUT THE
AUTHORS

Gay Hendricks is the author of more than 25 books dealing with personal and relationship transformation, including *Conscious Loving* (co-authored with his wife, Kathlyn Hendricks, Ph.D.), *Learning to Love Yourself,* and *Conscious Living.* He received his Ph.D. in counseling psychology from Stanford University and taught for 21 years at the University of Colorado before founding The Hendricks Institute (**www.hendricks.com**). He and Kathlyn make their home in Ojai, California. They are also co-founders, along with Stephen Simon, of The Spiritual Cinema Circle.

Debbie DeVoe is a freelance writer who specializes in creating experiential exercises and making complex ideas easy to understand. She lives and works in Bozeman, Montana.

We hope you enjoyed this Hay House book. If you'd like to receive our online catalog featuring additional information on Hay House books and products, or if you'd like to find out more about the Hay Foundation, please contact:

Hay House, Inc., P.O. Box 5100, Carlsbad, CA 92018-5100
(760) 431-7695 or (800) 654-5126
(760) 431-6948 (fax) or (800) 650-5115 (fax)
www.hayhouse.com® • www.hayfoundation.org

———

Published in Australia by: Hay House Australia Pty. Ltd.,
18/36 Ralph St., Alexandria NSW 2015
Phone: 612-9669-4299 • *Fax:* 612-9669-4144
www.hayhouse.com.au

Published in the United Kingdom by: Hay House UK, Ltd.,
The Sixth Floor, Watson House, 54 Baker Street, London W1U 7BU
Phone: +44 (0)20 3927 7290 • *Fax:* +44 (0)20 3927 7291
www.hayhouse.co.uk

Published in India by: Hay House Publishers India,
Muskaan Complex, Plot No. 3, B-2, Vasant Kunj, New Delhi 110 070
Phone: 91-11-4176-1620 • *Fax:* 91-11-4176-1630
www.hayhouse.co.in

———

Access New Knowledge.
Anytime. Anywhere.

Learn and evolve at your own pace
with the world's leading experts.

www.hayhouseU.com

BONUS CONTENT

Thank you for purchasing *The Power of a Single Thought* by Gay Hendricks and Debbie DeVoe. This product includes a free download! To access this bonus content, please visit **www.hayhouse.com/download** and enter the Product ID and Download Code as they appear below.

Product ID: 8335

Download Code: audio

For further assistance, please contact Hay House Customer Care by phone: US (800) 654-5126 or INTL CC+(760) 431-7695 or visit www.hayhouse.com/contact.

Thank you again for your Hay House purchase. Enjoy!

Hay House, Inc. • P.O. Box 5100 • Carlsbad, CA 92018 • (800) 654-5126

The Power of a Single Thought Audio Download Track List

1. Bonus Content

Caution: This audio program features meditation/visualization exercises that render it inappropriate for use while driving or operating heavy machinery.

Publisher's note: Hay House products are intended to be powerful, inspirational, and life-changing tools for personal growth and healing. They are not intended as a substitute for medical care. Please use this audio program under the supervision of your care provider. Neither the author nor Hay House, Inc., assumes any responsibility for your improper use of this product.

Printed in the United States
by Baker & Taylor Publisher Services